Anger and Stress Management

Commanding Keys to Manage Anger, Stress, Diminish Anxiety and Raise Happiness

By

GoldInk Books

BEFORE YOU START READING, DOWNLOAD YOUR FREE DIGITAL ASSETS!

Be sure to visit the URL below on your computer or mobile device to access the free digital asset files that are included with your purchase of this book.

These digital assets will complement the material in the book and are referenced throughout the text.

DOWNLOAD YOURS HERE:

www.GoldInkBooks.com

© **Copyright 2021 by GoldInk Books - All rights reserved.**

This document is geared towards providing exact and reliable information in regard to the topic and issue covered. The publication is sold with the idea that the publisher is not required to render accounting, officially permitted, or otherwise, qualified services. If advice is necessary, legal or professional, a practiced individual in the profession should be ordered.

From a Declaration of Principles which was accepted and approved equally by a Committee of the American Bar Association and a Committee of Publishers and Associations.

In no way is it legal to reproduce, duplicate, or transmit any part of this document in either electronic means or in printed format. Recording of this publication is strictly prohibited and any storage of this document is not allowed unless with written permission from the publisher. All rights reserved.

The information provided herein is stated to be truthful and consistent, in that any liability, in terms of inattention or otherwise, by any usage or abuse of any policies, processes, or directions contained within is the solitary and utter responsibility of the recipient reader. Under no circumstances will any legal responsibility or blame be held against the publisher for any reparation, damages, or monetary loss due to the information herein, either directly or indirectly.

Respective authors own all copyrights not held by the publisher.

The information herein is offered for informational purposes solely and is universal as so. The presentation of the information is without contract or any type of guarantee assurance.

The trademarks that are used are without any consent, and the publication of the trademark is without permission or backing by the trademark owner. All trademarks and brands within this book are for clarifying purposes only and are owned by the owners themselves, not affiliated with this document.

Table of Contents

INTRODUCTION 7

CHAPTER 1: HEART OF ANGER AND STRESS 11

1.1 Causes of Anger...13

1.2 Causes of Stress 18

CHAPTER 2: CRIPPLING NATURE OF STRESS AND ANGER 27

2.1 Inside Stress 27

2.2 Inside Anger..36

CHAPTER 3: MANAGING AN ANGRY BRAIN 43

3.1 Are You Ready for a Change?...45

3.2 Exploring Yourself 46

3.3 Identifying Triggers 48

3.4 Being Aware of Anger Warning Signs..........................50

3.5 Learning to Calm Yourself 51

3.6 Expressing Your Anger in a Healthy Way 58

CHAPTER 4: MANAGING A STRESSED BRAIN 67

4.1 Identifying Source of Stress..69

4.2 Being Aware of Stress Signs 71

4.3 Finding Response for a Quick Stress Relief 72

4.4 Making Use of the 4 A's of Stress Management...........77

4.5 Making Time for Fun and Relaxation 81

4.6 Learning to Connect with Others 82

4.7 Making Quick Stress Relief a Habit 82

4.8 Managing Your Time Better 84

4.9 Making Exercise a Habit 85

4.10 Changing Your Lifestyle 86

CHAPTER 5: ACTIVITIES FOR KEEPING ANGER AND STRESS AT BAY 89

5.1 Activities for Hot Heads 89

5.2 Activities for Stress Heads 95

CONCLUSION 100

Introduction

Have you caught something contagious?

It depends. Do stress and anger keep interfering with enjoying your life? Then yes, you have caught a contagious sickness, and it has found a home in you.

Stress is contagious, an umbrella term for negative feelings such as anxiety, frustration, and worry. All emotions, including anger, are contagious. You can "catch" them from other people, just like a normal cold. They can make you feel wiped out, just like a virus.

Like you, I was also part of more than one-third of the world population feeling stressed, worried, or angry. If you have one of the three, the rest of the two are usually inevitable. This crushing triangle hit me in my early twenties, and I was out of place until the day of realization finally came.

I was at my parents' house over the weekend. My aunt was also visiting with her little kids. I was standing in the kitchen sipping my morning coffee when I got a text message from a friend that our supervisor had rejected our project proposal that I was passionate about. As soon as I got the news, a wave of rage spurred up in my body, and before I knew it, the cup in my hand was in pieces on the floor. I was so self-immersed that I did not realize that my three-year-old niece was coming towards me. I vividly remember the fear in her eyes to this day as she cried her heart out. That day, I realized that I was fuelling up this unnecessary fire inside me that was hurting people around me, and I was never the one to hurt anyone. This anger had not even spared its caretaker.

If you are a victim of this devastating trio, you must already know how hard it makes your life. You carry a constant pain in the head as you go about your day. You cannot focus on your studies, work, family, and friends because your mind keeps wandering around for something to stress about. It gets difficult to carry out your daily tasks and make reasonable judgments. You are half attentive and your mind exaggerates the situation at hand and sends you into overdrive, pushing your loved ones away. You lose the sense of your appetite. Taking care of yourself seems like too much work. You feel overwhelmed most of the days and feel like you lack control of your life. You know what the problem is, but you do not know how to make it better. Most importantly, you do not know how to feel better.

Furthermore, the coronavirus pandemic 2019 has been a public health and psychological emergency. Living in isolation, job loss, financial struggle, changes in our daily lives, and mourning over the death of a loved one all can negatively impact many people's mental health and well-being. Nearly 2 in 3 Americans are experiencing stress which multiplies its harmful effects in the form of anxiety, anger, fear, and more. This situation has made anger and stress management even more complicated.

This book that I have put together is a genuine effort to help you live a better life away from the dangerous uncontrollable anger and stress ride. This book will help you understand the psychology behind your issues to finally give a reason for how you feel and how you act. You will get to know how anger and stress result in further complications. After giving complete knowledge about your problems, I will introduce you to the methods to manage your stress and anger, which will also help reduce your anxiety and boost your happiness. In the end, I will walk you through a collection of exercises to revitalize your life.

The first two chapters will build up a concept of your problems, and the next three chapters will be a practical guide towards anger and stress management.

Ordinary life stressors can have irreversible effects on your health, ranging from premature aging to heart disease to long-term impairment. According to a 2013 study by neuroscientists, even mild levels of stress can damage our ability to control our emotions, anger being a primary one. Intense emotions like anger can not only contribute to stress and anxiety but also memory loss. Holding anger in for long periods, turning inward, or exploding in wrath can all negatively affect your body. It even has the potential to shorten your life. Some people are predisposed to particular diseases, and continuous stress can exacerbate these conditions. Cancer, suicide, lung disease, and cirrhosis of the liver have all been related to stress.

Why should you believe anything I have to offer in this book? I am a certified psychotherapist. After helping myself come out of that dark headspace, I decided to help others going through the same experience. I am an expert on managing anger, stress, and relationships using proven techniques from mindfulness and neuroscience. I have both professional and personal knowledge on the subject. What you are about to read is something I wish I had to help me out. You do not have to surf the internet, getting yourself confused between lies and truth.

It is all here in one book.

I have to be honest with you it was not easy for me to get out of this state of mind, but in everybody's life, there comes a point where they wish they had tried harder to turn their life around, so let that point be today rather than tomorrow.

With my expertise and experiences, I have jotted down everything you need to know to help you prevent your anger and stress issues. Real-life examples and practices in this book will make your journey easier and effective.

Chapter 1: Heart of Anger and Stress

According to a 2018 study in the UK, 74% of people have felt overwhelmed or unable to cope because of their stress. In the last year, 42% of Americans polled claimed that they were angrier than they used to be in the previous year.

Due to stress, 46% of people said they ate too much or ate unhealthily. 29 percent indicated that they began or increased their drinking, while 16 percent reported that they began or increased their smoking. Depressed feelings were expressed by 51 percent of stressed people, while anxiety was recorded by 61 percent.

Stress and anger seem to grow like an epidemic in our society. Let me define these for you so you can get a better idea of what you are experiencing.

A feeling of bodily or emotional tension is referred to as stress. Any thought or event that makes you furious, annoyed, or nervous can trigger it. Your body's response to a demand or challenge is called stress. Stress can be good in small amounts, such as when it enables you to avoid danger or make a deadline. Stress can be harmful to your health if it lasts for a long time. Physical symptoms of stress include chest pain or a racing heart, aches and pains, trouble sleeping, exhaustion, dizziness, headaches, or shaking, muscle tension, high blood pressure, digestive problems, sexual troubles, and a weak immune system. Stress can cause mental and emotional symptoms like irritability, anxiety, depression, sadness, and panic attacks.

Anger is a negative emotion defined by hostility toward someone, or something you believe has wronged you on purpose. Excessive rage, on the other hand, can be problematic. Anger causes increased blood pressure and other physical changes, making it harder to think clearly and harming your physical and mental health. You may be having trouble managing your anger if you are verbally or physically abusing others, you are constantly irritated, feel out of control with your rage, frequently regret what you have said or done, and insignificant things upset you. According to a Harvard Medical School study, about 8% of teenagers have anger difficulties that would qualify them for a lifetime diagnosis of the intermittent explosive disorder. Individuals who have difficulty regulating their anger or who experience anger in the ways that are out of nature for them can have different types of anger disorders.

It is possible that people who are feeling passive anger are unaware that they are angry. Your emotions may manifest as sarcasm, apathy, or meanness when you are experiencing passive anger. You might engage in self-destructive habits like alienating friends and family, skipping school or work, or underperforming in professional or social circumstances. Outsiders will think that you are deliberately sabotaging yourself, even if you do not understand it or cannot justify your behavior.

Aggressive anger victims are usually conscious of their feelings, albeit they may not always grasp the source of their rage. Because dealing with the true issues is too tough, they sometimes channel violent and angry outbursts to scapegoats. Aggressive rage can take the form of volatile or retaliatory anger, which can lead to physical harm to property and other people.

Internalized anger can include depressing and dark thoughts as well as harsh self-talk. Punishing yourself is typically related to interior anger, such as depriving yourself of the activities you enjoy, such as watching television or exercising. It may also imply depriving yourself of basic necessities such as food and water.

Anger and stress have a prominent mutual friend among many others, and that is anxiety, and the reason for this mutual friend is that anger and stress are strongly interconnected. Let's discuss the causes of anger and stress separately to make our understanding better on the subject.

1.1 Causes of Anger

Once, a snake made its way into a carpentry shop. It slipped over a saw and was slightly injured as a result. Suddenly, it turned and bit the saw, and the snake's mouth was severely hurt! Then, not knowing what was going on and believing the saw was attacking "him," it proceeded to roll around the saw, attempting to suffocate it with its entire body by squeezing it with all of its strength, but it was killed by the saw. We may react angrily in order to punish those who have hurt us, but we soon realize that we are hurting ourselves. Unhealthy anger is destructive, and we need to figure out the causes behind our anger so we can cater to it.

- **Childhood and Upbringing**

    Many people receive messages about anger as youngsters that make it more difficult to manage as adults. For example, you may have grown up believing that acting out your anger aggressively or violently is always acceptable, and as a result, you have never learned how to effectively manage your angry feelings. This could suggest that you have angry outbursts anytime you do not like someone's behavior or are in an unpleasant scenario.

    You may have been raised to believe that you should never complain, and you may have been punished as a child for expressing anger. This could indicate that you have a tendency to repress your anger, which can lead to a long-term problem in which you respond improperly to new situations that you are unfamiliar with. If you do not feel like you can let go of your rage in a healthy way, you could take it out on yourself. Children should be reprimanded solely for their problematic behavior, not for their emotions. If parents respond otherwise on a regular basis, children will, unfortunately, learn to suppress their emotions and internalize their feelings. On the surface, this will appear to be nice, complying behavior; nevertheless, it is simply a coping strategy that kids adopt in order to please parents and escape parental disapproval (indeed, the majority of children will do almost everything to avoid parental disapproval).

When parents shut off' their children by punishing their emotions, they are actually developing a shame-ridden and emotionally suffocated child, rather than a well-mannered, cooperative little person who is more likely to develop future emotional & relational problems). The child will learn that some emotions are "inappropriate," "bad," or "destructive," and will progressively learn to repress those emotions, first around you, then with others.

They will also learn that certain aspects of themselves must be 'hidden' and rejected by you and others. All of this will result in a lack of emotional regulation and a notion that they are unable to withstand powerful or painful emotions (this is very problematic indeed, as these factors often play a role in self-harming and adolescent suicidal behaviors). These children will eventually learn to fear their emotions and to cope with them in ineffective or even dangerous ways. You may have witnessed your parents' or other adults' out-of-control anger and learned to associate anger with harmful and dangerous behavior. This could indicate that you are now fearful of your own anger and are hesitant to express your thoughts when anything irritates you. Those sensations may later resurface at an unrelated moment, making it difficult to explain. An individual, who suffers from Angrophobia, or the fear of anger, is terrified of becoming angry since their anger is often out of control. Although Angrophobia does not always have a clear cause, it is almost always linked to a traumatic event in the past. People who grew up with angry parents or who were subjected to child abuse may be more likely to develop this fear.

Angrophobia may be more common in those who have been penalized for expressing anger. Self-doubt and even self-loathing might result from suppressing these feelings. Those who repress their emotions are more likely to snap at some point, dumping their pent-up feelings on themselves or others in disastrous ways.

- **Past Events**

    If you have ever been in a scenario that made you furious, such as abuse, trauma, or bullying (as a child or more recently as an adult), and you were not able to express your anger safely at the time, you may still be dealing with those angry feelings now. This could indicate that you are now finding certain situations very difficult and prone to get enraged.

    Your current anger may be tied to a former event as well as the current situation, implying that the level of anger you are experiencing now reflects your previous situation. Being conscious of this can help us develop safer and less distressing ways to respond to problems in the present.

    Unfortunately, recollections of things we would rather forget to appear to be more intense than good memories. Anger, for example, might occupy your thoughts in ways that seem far more consuming and powerful than the delightful recollection of a former loving connection in reaction to a stimulus in the present that evokes an emotional memory. Anger makes you want to defend yourself, retaliate, or redress what has been left unaddressed.

Because anger is a basic component of the human survival reaction, it is usually a central characteristic of a survivor's response to trauma. Anger aids people in coping with life's challenges by providing us with more energy to persevere in the face of adversity. Uncontrolled rage, on the other hand, can lead to a feeling of being out of control of oneself and cause a slew of issues in the life of PTSD sufferers. High levels of rage, according to one view of anger and trauma, are linked to a basic survival impulse. Anger is a natural reaction to dread, situations that appear unfair, and feelings of being out of control or victimized when first confronted with a serious threat.

It can aid survival by directing all of a person's attention, cognition, brain activity, and action onto survival. Recent research has found that in people with PTSD, these responses to intense fear might become "stuck." This may trigger a survival mode reaction, in which the person is more likely to react to stimuli with "full activation," as if they were life or self-threatening. Individuals with PTSD experience an immediate response of impatience and rage, which can cause major problems at work and at home. It might have an effect on how people feel about themselves and their positions in society.

Anger can also be a legitimate response to betrayal or losing basic trust in people, according to another line of research, particularly in cases of interpersonal exploitation or violence.

- **Current Circumstances**

    If you are struggling with a lot of other challenges in your life right now, you might find yourself becoming irritated at irrelevant things more easily than usual. If you are furious about something but do not know how to express or resolve it, you can find yourself expressing your anger at other times. Anger can be an aspect of sadness as well. It can be extremely tough to manage all of the conflicting emotions you may be experiencing after losing someone close to you.

I hope you have understood where your anger comes from. If not, maybe stress is the culprit behind your anger issues, but where does stress come from?

1.2 Causes of Stress

Anxiety and stress are like a glass of water. Everything is okay if you think about them for a brief time. When you think about them for a long time, they start to make you feel uneasy. And if you think about them all the time, you will feel paralyzed, unable to move forward or accomplish anything.

I can also add to this analogy for you. What happens if we add more water to the glass? What if you completely fill the glass? Things get shaky. You are having trouble concentrating, and water is spilling out. You are now concerned about the water that has spilled as well. You are having trouble paying attention and keeping the glass, still if someone is talking to you right now. You have also been told that spilling is terrible and that you should be ashamed of yourself for allowing your emotions (water) to spill. So, now you cannot concentrate, you are embarrassed, and your arm hurts.

You can be stressed by a variety of factors. For the seventh year in a row, money and job were the top two sources of stress for adults in the United States, according to the 2015 Stress in America poll. Family duties, personal health issues, health problems impacting the family, and the economy were all common contributors. Let's explore the causes in a bit more detail.

- **Financial Problems**

  In 2015, the American Psychological Association found out that 72 percent of Americans were anxious about money at least once in the preceding month. Money was a substantial cause of stress for the majority of research participants, with 77 percent expressing serious financial anxiety.

  Financial stress can manifest itself in a variety of ways, including:

  > Getting into a financial dispute with family and friends

  > Fear of opening mail or picking up the phone

  > Feeling remorseful for splurging on non-essentials

  > Worrying and being concerned about money

  Long-term financial stress causes distress, which can lead to high blood pressure, headaches, chest pain, upset stomach, a general feeling of ill health, and insomnia. Financial stress has also been connected to anxiety, depression, skin disorders, arthritis, and diabetes.

- **Personal Relationships**

We might have people in our lives who bring us stress. It could be a close relative, a romantic partner, a friend, or a coworker. Toxic people exist in every aspect of our lives, and the stress we experience as a result of these connections can have a negative impact on our physical and mental health.

In romantic relationships, there are many sources of stress, and when couples are continually under strain, the relationship is at risk of failing.

The following are some of the most common relationship stressors:

> - Too preoccupied to spend time together and share duties
> - Due to busyness, health issues, and a variety of other factors, intimacy and sex have become increasingly rare.
> - Abuse or control.
> - Ineffective communication
> - Divorce

Personal relationship stress symptoms are comparable to general stress symptoms and may include physical health and sleep issues, depression, and anxiety. You can also find yourself avoiding or fighting with the person or easily agitated by their presence. Personal connection stress is sometimes linked to our interactions with people on social media platforms like Facebook. For example, social media encourages you to compare yourself to others, which can lead to feelings of inadequacy and stress. It also facilitates bullying.

- **Workplace Problems**

    According to (CDC) the Centers for Disease Control and Prevention, Americans today spend 8% more hours at work than they did 20 years ago, and 13% have a second job. At least 40% of those polled say that their jobs are stressful, and 26% say that they are frequently burned out.

    Too much work, dissatisfaction with a job or career, job insecurity, and disagreements with a boss and/or coworkers are just some of the factors that can lead to job stress.

    Putting your career first can have a negative impact on many elements of your life, including mental and physical health and personal relationships, whether you are stressed about a specific project or feel unfairly treated at work.

    A person's psychological makeup, general health, personal life, and the amount of emotional support they receive outside of work all play a part in work stress.

    Physical and psychological manifestations of work-related stress include:

- Depression
- Anxiety
- Difficulty concentrating
- Indecisiveness
- Fatigue
- Heart palpitations
- Headache
- Mood swings
- Stomach problems
- Muscle tension and pain

Some people may feel overwhelmed and have difficulty coping, which can have an impact on their conduct. People who are stressed at work may develop:

- Disinterest
- Diminished creativity and initiative
- Not satisfying work performance
- Increased sick days
- Lower levels of patience
- Isolation
- Problems with personal relationships
- Increased levels of frustration

- **Daily Life Stressors**

   Our daily annoyances are our daily stressors. Misplacing keys, being late, and forgetting to carry a crucial item with you when leaving the house are all their examples. These are usually small setbacks, but if they occur frequently enough, they can become a cause of anxiety, negatively impacting physical and/or psychological health.

   The stress of being overworked is becoming increasingly widespread. People are busier than ever, which add a lot of stress to their life. In other instances, such as needing to work a second job, busyness is unavoidable. Other times, it is out of shame or a desire to avoid disappointing people. Due to a lack of time, people may be unable to say "no" and thus have little time for themselves, or they may neglect their own basic requirements, such as eating well and exercising.

Sometimes the source of stress is internal rather than external. How, you will ask? Let me explain:

- **Perception and Attitude**

    The way you see the world or a certain event can influence whether or not it triggers stress. If your television set is stolen, for example, and you adopt a negative attitude, "You will feel lot less agitated if you think, "It is okay, my insurance company will pay for a new one." than if you think, "My TV is gone, and I will never get it back!" What if the robbers return to my home to steal from me once more?" People who believe they that mare doing a good job at work will also be less stressed by a large future project than those who believe that they are incompetent.

- **Uncertainty and Fear**

    When you hear about violence, global warming, and dangerous chemicals on the news on a regular basis, it might make you feel anxious, especially if you feel powerless to stop it. Even while disasters are normally infrequent occurrences, their extensive coverage in the media may give the impression that they are more common than they are. Fears can also be more personal, such as worrying that you would not be able to finish a project at work or that you would not be able to pay your bills this month.

- **Change**

  Any major life transition, even a pleasant event like a wedding or a job promotion, may be stressful. More negative situations, such as a divorce, a large financial setback, or a family death, can be huge sources of stress.

- **Unrealistic Expectations**

  No one is without flaws. If you expect to do everything perfectly all of the time, you will be stressed out when things do not go as planned.

These were the main causes of stress and anger. In the next chapter, we will study how bad stress and anger can be for you if left unmanaged.

Chapter 2: Crippling Nature of Stress and Anger

Physical dangers posed a significant source of stress in the caveman era, requiring humans to react quickly and aggressively. The body responded by producing a barrage of 'stress' chemicals. The caveman's stress response made him ready to react to danger right away.

Stressors and triggers for anger in today's world are more likely to be psychological and last a long time, e.g., financial worries, work-related stress, chronic illnesses, interpersonal relationships. They can, however, set off your body's aggressive, emotional response, which can have a variety of detrimental effects over time on the body's systems, including the cardiovascular, brain, immune system, musculoskeletal, digestive system, and so on. We will learn about the psychology of stress and anger more in the next sections. Let's get started.

2.1 Inside Stress

Stress is a biological reaction to events that occur in your life. When you view a situation as stressful, your brain's hypothalamus activates the stress response. It all starts with a communication sent to the pituitary gland. The adrenal glands receive a message from the pituitary gland. On top of your kidneys are the adrenal glands. The stress hormone cortisol is then released by these glands. Your breathing and heart rate speed up, and your blood pressure rises as a result of the stress response. Your liver breaks down molecules and releases more glucose into the blood with the help of cortisol.

An increase in blood sugar levels gives the body extra energy. For the fight or flight reaction, this is crucial. The boost in energy allows you to flee or deal with stressful circumstances. It also aids the body's recovery from the procedure.

People can learn to cope with modest levels of stress over time. When you repeatedly experience a stressful event, your prefrontal cortex, or brain's command center, detects the stressor and notifies your hypothalamus that the stress reaction is supposed to be brief. Cortisol levels in the body remain high when exposed to frequent or long-term stress.

What happens, though, if your body is exposed to high quantities of stress chemicals for a long time? After a while, the stress becomes unhealthy. Cortisol levels that are too high start to wear down the brain and other body systems over time. This form of brain injury has been linked to a variety of health issues, including depression and anxiety disorders, memory loss, and dementia.

So, keep in mind that while some stress is beneficial, too much stress can be damaging over time! Now I am going to explain some reasons why you need to manage your stress.

Effects of stress

Your nervous system cannot differentiate between physical and emotional dangers. When you are stressed out about a disagreement with a companion, a work deadline, or a stack of bills, your body can react as if you are in a truly life-or-death situation. The more your emergency stress system will be activated, the easier it will be to trigger it, making it more difficult to deactivate. In case, you are frequently stressed out, as many of us are in today's demanding society, your body may be in a condition of high stress much of the time.

Chronic stress has the potential to disrupt every part of your life, including your emotions, actions, cognitive abilities, and physical health. There is no part of the human body that is immune. However, because people react to stress in different ways, the effects of stress might differ:

- **How Stress Takes a Toll on the Body?**

  Your body is at risk due to stress in the following ways:

  > **Cardiovascular System:**
  >
  > When you are stressed, your heart beats faster. Stress hormones stimulate your blood vessels to contract, allowing more oxygen to get to your muscles, giving you more power to perform. This, however, boosts your blood pressure.
  >
  > As a result, chronic or frequent stress causes your heart to work too hard for too long. Your chances of suffering a stroke or heart attack increase when your blood pressure rises.

  > **Digestive System:**
  >
  > When you are stressed, your liver creates more blood sugar (glucose) to give you an energy boost. If you are under a lot of stress, your body might not be able to handle the extra glucose. Chronic stress has been linked to an increased risk of type 2 diabetes.
  >
  > Hormone surges, quick breathing, and a faster heart rate can all cause stomach problems. Due to an increase in stomach acid, you are more likely to have heartburn or acid reflux. Although stress does not cause ulcers, it can raise your risk of developing them and make existing ulcers worse.

Stress can also cause diarrhea or constipation by altering the way food travels through your body. You may also feel nauseated, vomit, or have a stomachache.

➤ **Reproductive System:**

Stress can cause a man's testosterone levels to plummet if he is exposed to it for an extended period of time. This can induce erectile dysfunction or impotence by interfering with sperm production. Male reproductive organs, e.g., testes and prostate, may be more susceptible to infection as a result of chronic stress.

Stress can disrupt a woman's menstrual cycle. It can cause periods to become irregular, heavier, or more uncomfortable. Menopause's physical effects might be exacerbated by chronic stress.

➤ **Muscular System:**

When you are anxious, your muscles contract up to protect yourself from injury. They usually release after you rest, but if you are always stressed, your muscles may never get the opportunity to relax. Headaches, shoulder pain, back pain, and general aches are all symptoms of tight muscles. This might lead to an unhealthy cycle in which you quit exercising and rely on pain medication to feel better.

- **Immune System:**
  Stress boosts the immune system, which is beneficial in emergency situations. This stimulation can help in the prevention of infections and the healing of wounds. Hormones released due to stress, on the other hand, impair your immune system and lessen your body's reaction to external invaders over time. Chronically stressed people are more vulnerable to viral diseases such as the flu and the common cold, as well as other infections. Stress can also lengthen the time you take to heal from an illness or accident.

- **Insomnia:**
  Stress causes insomnia, which is a frequent sleep disorder. Insomnia is characterized by chronic problems with sleep initiation, maintenance, consolidation, or overall quality of sleep. People with insomnia experience extreme daytime sleepiness, weariness, irritability, and other impairments when they are up, despite having enough time permitted for sleep on a given night and sleeping in a pleasant area. According to current statistics, 10-30% of adults suffer from sleeplessness.

- **Obesity:**
  While short-term stress might lead to a loss of appetite, long-term stress can have the opposite

impact. In the short term, stress stimulates the brain to create the corticotrophin-releasing hormone, which suppresses hunger. Signals are delivered to the adrenal glands during times of stress, triggering the synthesis of adrenalin, which temporarily suppresses any desire to eat as part of the fight-or-flight reaction. On the other hand, chronic stress stimulates the release of a hormone called cortisol. This hormone boosts a person's hunger, and if the stress does not go away, cortisol and appetite levels stay high.

- **How Stress Takes a Toll on the Brain and Behavior?**

Stress affects your brain in the following ways:

> **Brain Structure:**

> Experiments also demonstrated that long-term changes in the structure and function of the brain could result from chronic stress. The brain's grey matter, which is responsible for higher-order thinking such as decision-making and problem-solving, is made up of neurons and support cells. However, the brain also contains "white matter," which is made up of all the axons that communicate information with other parts of the brain. The fatty, white layer known as myelin that envelopes the axons that speed up the electrical signals needed to transfer information throughout the brain gives white matter its name. The

overproduction of myelin found by the researchers in the presence of chronic stress does not simply cause a short-term shift in the balance between white and grey matter; it can also cause long-term structural abnormalities in the brain.

The researcher behind these trials, Psychologist Daniela Kaufer, believes that based on the patterning of white matter you get early in life, you are constructing a brain that's either resilient or very sensitive to mental disorders.

➤ **Brain Shrinkage:**
Stress can cause shrinkage in parts of the brain related to emotion regulation, metabolism, and memory, even in otherwise healthy people. While many people associate negative outcomes with sudden, intense stress caused by life-altering events (such as a car accident, natural disaster, or the death of a loved one), researchers believe that everyday stress, which we all seem to face, can contribute to a variety of mental disorders over time.

Researchers from Yale University studied 100 healthy people who shared information on stressful experiences in their life in one study. The researchers discovered that stress resulted in less grey matter in the prefrontal cortex, a brain region associated with self-control and emotions.

Chronic, everyday stress seems to have little effect on brain volume on its own, but it appears to render people more sensitive to brain shrinkage when faced with extreme, catastrophic stresses.

Distinct types of stress have different effects on the brain. Emotional awareness is affected by recent stressful experiences (job loss, automobile accidents). Mood centers are more affected by traumatic experiences (death of a loved one, significant sickness).

> **Killing Brain Cells:**

Researchers have discovered that a single socially stressful event can cause new neurons to die in the hippocampus of the brain. The hippocampus is a brain area that is strongly linked to emotion, memory, and learning. It is also one of two areas of the brain where neurogenesis, or the development of new brain cells, happens all the time.

The researchers experimented by putting young rats in a cage with two adult rats for 20 minutes. The baby rat was subsequently subjected to aggressiveness from the cage's more experienced members. The cortisol levels of the young rats were found to be up to six times greater than those of rats who had not undergone a stressful social encounter.

Further investigation found that, whereas young rats exposed to stress created the same number of new neurons as those who had not been exposed to stress, the number of nerve cells was significantly reduced a week later. Stress does not appear to affect the production of new neurons, but it does affect the survival of those cells.

- **Depression:**
- Chronic, or long-term, stress can be bad on its own, but it can also lead to depression, a mood condition that causes you to feel gloomy and uninterested in activities that you normally enjoy. Depression can have an impact on your appetite, sleep patterns, and capacity to focus. A substantial stressor, such as a divorce event a significant financial shift, is a major stressor that throws the psyche off balance. According to a researcher, if you keep increasing your stress levels, something will happen, and the most common outcome is depression.

- **Anxiety:**

- Corticotropin and cortisol hormones may increase anxiety and contribute to mood problems if stress levels do not decrease. Researchers laced the mice's drinking water with corticosterone in a study. They were able to avoid stressing the mice by not injecting them. The laced water was given to some mice for 17 or 18 days, simulating long-term stress hormone exposure. The other mice, on the other hand, only received the boosted water for one day. The mice were given two tests with no training to prepare them for them. Mice in a dark area of a cage were given the opportunity to explore a bright, open part of the cage in one experiment. The mice who consumed the tainted water on a daily basis were more cautious about entering the open area. The reluctance was regarded as anxiousness by the researchers.

If you have had stress for some time, you can relate to at least some of the above problems. Now let's try to understand the anger.

2.2 Inside Anger

Anger manifests in our bodies as well as our intellect, much like other emotions. When we feel furious, our bodies go through a complicated set of physiological (body) events. Emotions begin in our brains' amygdala, which is two almond-shaped structures. The amygdala is the portion of the brain that detects dangers to our well-being and issues an alarm when hazards are detected, prompting us to take protective measures. The amygdala is so good at warning us about dangers that it gets us reacting before the cortex (the part of the brain that deals with intellect and judgment) can verify if our reaction is sensible. In other words, our brains are constructed to compel us to act before we can fully comprehend the ramifications of our actions.

This is not a justification for terrible behavior; people can and do manage their aggressive tendencies, and with practice, you can as well. Instead, it indicates that correctly managing anger is a taught ability rather than something we are born with. Your body's muscles tense up as you become enraged. Catecholamines, which are neurotransmitter chemicals, are produced in your brain, generating a burst of energy that can last for several minutes. The typical outraged impulse to take quick protective action is the result of this burst of energy.

Your heart rate, blood pressure, and breathing rate all increase at the same moment. Increased blood flow to your limbs and extremities prepares you for physical activity, which may cause your face to flush. Your focus narrows to the source of your rage. Nothing else will be able to hold your attention for long. Additional brain neurotransmitters and hormones (including adrenaline and noradrenaline) are released in rapid succession, resulting in an arousal state that lasts for a long time. You are all set to fight now.

Although your emotions can spiral out of control, your prefrontal cortex, which is positioned directly beneath your brow, can keep them in check. The prefrontal cortex is in charge of judgment if the amygdala is in charge of emotion. Emotions can be turned off by the left prefrontal cortex. It acts as a supervisor, ensuring that everything is in order. Learning how to help your prefrontal cortex take control of your amygdala so you can manage how you react to anger feelings is the first step in gaining control over your anger.

Now let's dive into the reasons why you should make use of your left prefrontal cortex.

Effects of Anger

Anger is a powerful emotion that has behavioral manifestations. It can be a crucial tool for survival, but it can also cause substantial problems in the long run by knocking the mind's linked with thinking, feeling, behavior, and relationships. It is a forceful, uncomfortable, and awkward reaction to what you think is a provocation, harm, or danger. When personal boundaries are violated, anger is triggered. Anger is, by nature, a warning signal to defend oneself from fear, sadness, or suffering, either cognitively, behaviorally, or physically, from an externally harmful exposure through action chosen of one's own volition. Anger can have major effects on your life and behavior. Let's discuss them:

- **How Anger takes a Toll on the Body?**

  Your body is at risk due to anger in the following ways:

  > **Heart Problems:**
  > Most harmful effect of anger is on your heart health. According to a clinical psychiatry instructor, the risk of suffering a heart attack doubles in the two hours following an angry outburst. Moreover, it is researched that heart disease is linked to repressed anger when you express it indirectly or go to tremendous lengths to control it. According to one study, those who have anger proneness as a personality attribute have twice the risk of cardiovascular disease as their less angry counterparts.

➢ Immune System:

If you are mad all the time, you just might find yourself feeling sick more often. In one study, Harvard University scientists found that in healthy people, simply recalling an angry experience from their past caused a six-hour dip in levels of the antibody immunoglobulin A, the cells' first line of defense against infection. Moreover, according to an Ohio State University study, people who had less control over their anger healed wounds more slowly. Researchers gave blisters to 98 people and discovered that individuals who had less control over their anger, healed slower after eight days. Furthermore, throughout the blistering operation, those subjects had higher levels of cortisol (a stress hormone), implying that they were also more agitated by stressful events.

➢ Respiratory System:

Even if you do not smoke, being a persistently angry and hostile person might harm your lungs. Using a hostility scale scoring method to quantify anger levels and examine any changes in the men's lung function, a group of Harvard University scientists studied 670 men for eight years. The males who rated themselves as the most hostile had much lower lung capacity, increasing their risk of respiratory issues. Stress hormones, which are linked to feelings of anger, are thought to cause inflammation in the airways, according to the study.

➤ **Life Expectancy:**
A 17-year study by the University of Michigan discovered that couples who hold their anger in had lower life duration than those who express their anger openly. According to a study, stress is inextricably connected to overall health. You will live a shorter life if you are anxious and furious.

- **How Anger takes a Toll on the Brain and Behavior?**

Anger affects your brain in the following ways:

➤ **Anxiety:**
If you are a worrier, you should be aware that worry and anger can coexist. Anger can increase symptoms of a generalized anxiety disorder (GAD), a condition defined by excessive and uncontrollable worry that interferes with a person's everyday life, according to a 2012 study published in the journal Cognitive Behavior Therapy. Not only did patients with GAD have higher levels of anger, but hostility — particularly internalized, unexpressed anger — was linked to the severity of GAD symptoms.

➤ **Depression:**
Depression has been related in numerous studies to aggression and furious outbursts,

particularly in men. Passive rage is typical in depression, where you ruminate over something but never do anything about it. Anger issues in spouses and wives were explored in one study from the University of Washington: School of Nursing. Previous research has connected anger issues and depressive symptoms to all major causes of mortality, according to the researchers. Women, on the other hand, had a stronger link between anger and depressive symptoms, whereas men had a stronger link between anger and health issues.

- **Social Depravity:**
  Being angry all of the time has major social and emotional costs in addition to physical health implications. People who are hostile and angry are less likely to have good supportive relationships than those who are less hostile. Most importantly, persistent anger inhibits closeness in personal relationships and other family members are more guarded and less able to relax in unpleasant situations.

While this may not appear to be a bad fate to have, keep in mind that research constantly demonstrates that having healthy supportive relationships with family, friends, coworkers, and colleagues is critical for good health. Having the social support of one's peers might help one avoid mental troubles as well as significant health concerns like heart disease. When people have considerable social support, they are less likely to suffer from debilitating depression.

The physiological response to anger and arousal evolved to assist people in dealing with physical dangers. Physical aggression, on the other hand, is not always a suitable response in today's culture. This is especially true in the more public aspects of your life, such as your encounters at work. You will almost certainly be fired if you verbally assault your supervisor. Similarly, if you get out of your car and assault a driver who has cut you off, you could end up in court. Uncontrollable rage can lead to job loss, family separation, and even jail. Individuals who are unable to control their disruptive, violent conduct are more likely to face not only greater health risks but also major social problems.

I want to end this chapter on the note that stress and anger can destroy your physical and mental health. The next two chapters will help you eliminate this slow life-threatening poison from your life.

Chapter 3: Managing an Angry Brain

Managing your anger does not exempt you from being angry. Rather, it entails learning to recognize, manage, and express anger healthily and constructively. Anger management is a skill that can be learned by everyone. There is always space for improvement, even if you think you have got your anger under control.

Let's debunk some myths about anger before we move forward:

- **Anger Is a Bad Feeling**

    All of the primary emotions are necessary and hardwired into our brains. Stuffing them is not a good idea. One way the body communicates its requirements is through emotion. However, this does not imply that we must automatically react. We can respond more effectively and turn things around if we examine the feeling.

- **It is Okay to Blow Up**

    When we are angry, our minds may rationalize anything. When your mind is hijacked by anger, it is difficult to address problems. You can rationalize your angry outbursts by telling yourself, "She made me angry." It's not true, and it does not help matters.

- **Anger is all in your head.**

    Anger is more than just a mental state. Consider the last time you were truly enraged. Your heart rate probably raised, your face flushed, and your hands shook. This is because anger triggers a physiological response, which in turn fuels angry thoughts and aggressive actions. To reduce aggressive outbursts, you must learn to calm your body — and your thoughts.

- **Ignoring your anger will make it disappear.**

    Anger suppression is not good, either. Smiling to mask your dissatisfaction, rejecting your furious sentiments, or allowing others to treat you badly to keep the peace might cause your anger to spiral inward. In addition, suppressed rage has been linked to several physical and mental health problems, including hypertension and depression.

- **Some people are simply born with a bad temper that they cannot control.**

    Angry feelings are the result of experiences that are often unnoticed or forgotten and have nothing to do with the "reasons" we tell ourselves for being angry.

    You may believe that expressing your rage is healthy, that those around you are overly sensitive, that your anger is justifiable, or that you need to display your anger to gain respect. However, rage is much more likely to have a negative impact on how others see you, impair your judgment, and obstruct your success.

So let's learn the keys to tame your anger.

3.1 Are You Ready for a Change?

Choosing to take control of your anger rather than allowing it to control you necessitates a thorough examination of how you have been reacting when you are angry. Do you have a tendency to scream and yell or to say nasty, mean, and disrespectful things? Do you hurl objects, kick or punch walls, or break things? Do you want to hit someone, injure yourself, or push and shove other people around?

Most people who have problems controlling their temper do not wish to react in this way. They are embarrassed by their actions and believe that it does not reflect their true self, their best selves.

Everyone has the ability to change, but only when they want to. Consider what you will gain if you make a significant shift in how you handle your anger. Is it possible to have more self-respect? Is it possible to gain more respect from others? Spending less time irritated and frustrated? A more laid-back attitude toward life? It can assist in remembering why you want to make the change.

It is also a good idea to remind you that change takes time, effort, and patience. It is not going to happen all at once. Managing anger requires the development of new skills and responses. It helps to practice over and over again with any talent, such as learning the piano or playing basketball.

3.2 Exploring Yourself

Identifying the true source of your irritation will enable you to properly explain your anger, take positive action, and work toward a solution.

- **Is your anger concealing other emotions like humiliation, uncertainty, shame, hurt, or vulnerability?**

    If you find yourself reacting with anger in a variety of scenarios, it is likely that your fury is masking your genuine feelings. This is especially true if you grew up in a household where expressing emotions was frowned upon. You may find it difficult to acknowledge feelings other than anger as an adult.

- **Anger can also be a symptom of anxiety.**

    Your body engages the "fight or flight" response when you perceive a threat, real or imagined. The "fight" reaction is frequently manifested as rage or hostility in the case of the "fight" response. To alter your response, you must first identify the source of your anxiety or fear.

- **What you learned as a child may be the source of your anger issues.**

    You could think this is how anger is intended to be expressed if you see others in your family yell, strike each other, or throw items.

- **Anger can be a symptom of some underlying health issues.**

    It can be depression, trauma, or chronic stress (particularly in men).

There is more to your anger than meets the eye, according to these signs:

1. **You see opposing viewpoints as a personal challenge:** Do you think your way is always correct and become enraged when others disagree? If you have a strong need to be in charge or a weak ego, you may misinterpret other viewpoints as a threat to your authority rather than merely a different perspective.

2. **You may have a difficult time making compromises**: Is it difficult for you to understand other people's viewpoints and even more difficult for you to concede a point? If you grew up in a family where anger was out of control, you might recall how the person who was the most enraged got their way by being the loudest and demanding. Compromise can lead to frightening feelings of failure and vulnerability.

3. **You find it difficult to communicate feelings other than anger:** Do you take satisfaction in being tough and in command? Do you think you are immune to emotions like fear, remorse, or shame? Everyone has those feelings, so you could be masking them with rage. It is critical to reconnecting with your feelings if you are uncomfortable with diverse emotions, disengaged, or stuck on an angry one-note response to things.

3.3 Identifying Triggers

While stressful events do not justify anger, recognizing how they impact you can help you take control of your surroundings and avoid unneeded annoyance. Examine your daily routine to see if there are any activities, people, and times of day, places, or situations that make you irritated or furious.

Maybe every time you go out for drinks with a certain set of pals, you get into a fight. Alternatively, perhaps the traffic on your daily commute drives you insane. You might decide to reorganize your day to better manage your stress. Alternatively, you might practice anger control strategies before encountering situations that you normally find stressful. Doing these activities can help you prolong your fuse, which means you would not be triggered by a single frustrating experience.

You may believe that your anger is caused by external sources such as other people's callous actions or frustrating situations. However, anger issues have less to do with what happens to you and more to do with how you interpret and think about it.

The following are some common negative thought processes that cause and fuel anger:

1. **Overgeneralizing:** It can look like this:

    "You 'always' interrupt me."

    "You 'never' think about what I need."

    "' Everyone' looks down on me."

    "I am 'never' given the credit I am due."

2. **Obsessing over the words "should" and "must:"** Having a rigid picture of how a situation should or must unfold and being enraged when reality fails to match this ideal.

3. **Jumping to conclusions and interpreting people's minds:** Assuming you "know" what someone else is thinking or feeling and that they have done so on purpose to upset you, ignore your requests, or insult you.

4. **Collecting Straws:** Looking for things to be angry about while ignoring or brushing aside anything beneficial. Allowing tiny irritations to build up until you reach the "last straw" and explode, usually over something insignificant.

5. **Blaming:** It is always someone else's fault when something unpleasant happens or goes wrong. Instead of taking responsibility for your own life, you tell yourself, "Life isn't fair," or blame others for your troubles.

You may learn to reframe how you think about things after you discover the mental patterns that feed your anger. Consider this: What evidence do you have that the thought is correct? Is it possible that this is not the case? Is there a more optimistic, realistic perspective on a situation? What would I say to a friend who had these thoughts?

3.4 Being Aware of Anger Warning Signs

While it may appear that you become enraged without warning, your body does exhibit physical warning signs. You may take efforts to regulate your anger before it spirals out of control if you become aware of your own personal indicators that your temper is starting to boil. Pay attention to how your anger makes your body feel:

- Clenching your jaw or hands
- Knots in your stomach
- Feeling flushed or clammy
- Breathing faster
- Pacing or feel the need to walk around
- Headaches
- Having trouble concentrating
- "Seeing red"
- Tensing your shoulders
- Pounding heart

3.5 Learning to Calm Yourself

You can cope with your anger before it gets out of control if you know how to spot the warning signals that your temper is rising and anticipate your triggers. There are a variety of ways that can assist you in calming down and controlling your anger.

- Concentrate on the physical manifestations of anger. While it may seem paradoxical, paying attention to how your body feels when you are furious might help you manage your anger's emotional intensity.

- Learn to step away. Trying to win an argument or sticking it out in a bad scenario will just make you more enraged. When your anger is increasing, one of the finest things you can do is to get out of the situation as soon as possible.

- Take a break when a discussion becomes heated. If you feel like you are about to blow up, you should leave the meeting. If your children are bothering you, go for a walk. A time-out might be beneficial in calming your mind and body.

If you regularly have heated arguments with someone, such as a friend or family member, talk to them about the necessity of taking a break and restarting when you both are feeling calm. When you need to take a break, explain that you are not attempting to avoid unpleasant topics; instead, you are working on anger management.

When you are upset, it is impossible to have a meaningful talk or resolve a disagreement. When you are feeling more relaxed, you can continue the conversation or address the issue.

Setting a precise time and place to discuss the topic again can sometimes be beneficial. This gives your colleague, friend, or family member the assurance that the matter will be addressed — just at a later time.

- You can use a variety of relaxation activities to help you manage your anger. You have to work out which one works best for you. Two prominent ways for lowering tension are breathing exercises and progressive muscle relaxation.

  The best aspect is that both exercises may be completed in a short amount of time and with minimal effort. So, whether you are dissatisfied at work or angry about a dinner reservation, you can swiftly and easily let go of stress.

  It is crucial to keep in mind, too, that relaxation techniques take time to master. You might not think that they are effective at first, or you might wonder if they are going to work for you. They can, however, become your go-to tactics for anger management with practice.

- You get a burst of energy when you are angry. Engaging in physical activity is one of the best ways to put that surge to good use. Working out, whether it is a brisk stroll or a trip to the gym can help you relieve stress. Regular exercise also aids in the decompression process. Aerobic activity reduces tension, which may help you cope better with frustration. Exercising also assists you to de-clutter your mind. You might discover that after a long run or a strenuous workout, you have a better understanding of what is bothering you.

- Make use of your senses. To swiftly reduce stress and chill down, engage your senses of smell, sight, hearing, taste, and touch. Looking at a favorite photo, relishing a cup of tea, or touching a pet are all good options.

- Humor and playfulness may help you lighten the mood, smooth over disagreements, reframe difficulties, and keep things in perspective when things get tense. When you are feeling irritated in a scenario, try a little lighthearted comedy. It can help you communicate your message without raising the other person's defense or hurting their feelings.

It is critical, however, that you laugh with the other person rather than at them. Avoid sarcasm and derogatory humor. If you are unsure, start with self-deprecating humor. We all admire folks who can gently mock their own shortcomings. After all, we are all fallible, and we are all prone to making errors. So, instead of getting furious or creating a fight because you made a mistake at work or spilled coffee all over yourself, try making a joke about it. The only person you risk insulting is yourself if the joke falls flat or is delivered incorrectly. A potential confrontation can even become a chance for better connection and intimacy when humor and play are used to relieve tension and hostility. Sarcasm, however, should be avoided because it might hurt feelings and make things worse.

- Manage your thoughts. Your anger is fueled by angry thoughts. "I can't stand it," you might think. "This traffic delay is going to spoil everything," you'll think to yourself. Reframe your thoughts when you find yourself thinking about things that make you angry. Instead, consider the facts and offer something like, "Every day, millions of cars are on the road." There will be traffic jams sometimes." Staying calmer can be as simple as focusing on the facts without throwing in terrible prophecies or twisted exaggerations. You might also come up with a mantra that you can repeat to drown out the thoughts that are fueling your anger. Using the phrase, "I'm fine, "Remain calm," or "This is not helpful," repeatedly can assist you in minimizing or reducing furious thoughts.

- Tension points can be stretched or massaged. If you are tensing your shoulders, for example, roll them or softly massage your neck and scalp.

- Count to ten slowly. Concentrate on counting to allow your rational thinking to catch up with your emotions. Start counting again if you still feel out of control when you get to ten.

- Try to engage in some activity. Anger is fueled by ruminating about a difficult situation. If you have had a difficult day at work, for example, reviewing everything that went wrong all evening will leave you locked in a rut. Changing the channel in your brain and focusing on something else entirely may be the best way to relax. It is not always effective to tell yourself,

"Don't worry about that." Distracting yourself with an activity is the easiest method to mentally shift gears. Do something that needs your whole attention and makes it harder for angry or negative ideas to enter your mind.

Deep cleaning the kitchen, playing with the kids, and weeding the garden are just a few examples. Find an activity to keep yourself occupied so you do not linger on the things that are bothering you. Then your body and mind will be able to relax.

- Try talking to a friend. Talking out an issue or expressing your concerns to someone who has a calming influence on you could be beneficial. However, keep in mind that venting can backfire. Complaining about your boss, listing all the reasons you dislike someone, or whining about all the apparent injustices may add fuel to the fire. It is a frequent misperception that you need to express your anger in order to feel better.

   However, research shows that you don't need to "get your rage out." When you are furious, smashing objects, for example, may make you even angrier. As a result, it is critical to use caution when employing this coping technique. If you are going to talk to a friend about something, make sure you are working on a solution or lessening your anger rather than just venting. It is unjust to rely on them as a sounding board. Instead, you might discover that talking about something other than the scenario that makes you furious is the greatest approach to employ this strategy.

- Visualize yourself being calm. This tip needs you to put your new breathing methods into practice. Close your eyes. Visualize your calmness after taking a couple of deep breaths. Now imagine your body relaxed while you work through a stress-inducing situation while remaining focused and calm. When you create a mental demonstration of what it feels like to be calm, you can turn to it when you are feeling worried.

- Challenge your thinking. Having irrational ideas that do not make sense is a part of being furious or worried. These are usually the "worst-case scenario" thoughts. You may get stuck in the "what if" cycle, which can lead to you sabotaging important aspects of your life. Pause and ask yourself the following questions when you have one of these thoughts:

  - Is this a possibility?
  - Is this a reasonable assumption?
  - What is the worst situation that could happen in reality? Is it something I can handle?

- We have all misinterpreted a friend's or partner's remark, especially when we are hungry, fatigued, or stressed. So, taking a moment to consider the genuine motive of a seemingly cruel comment can rapidly calm a situation. When we get angry, our mind perceives someone as a threat, and we must defend ourselves, but sometimes we interpret things wrong or hear things incorrectly.

- It is easy to live in denial and refuse to admit your flaws. Take a minute to evaluate a perspective that is in your best interests if someone close to you suggests it before dismissing it outright and becoming furious. This will become easier over time if you have an attitude of ongoing improvement. Actively seek criticism; it will help you develop a thick skin and, in the process, give you a new perspective on things.

- Take a moment. Think about all the things you are thankful for. Instead of feeling that everything is wrong, recognize that you have a lot to be grateful for. This may help you manage your anger.

3.6 Expressing Your Anger in a Healthy Way

The problem is that we are not taught how to express ourselves in a healthy way, so we end up stuffing our emotions. We are either taught to completely avoid our feelings, or we have witnessed some extremely unpleasant expressions of anger, making even contemplating expressions seem terrifying. Whether the anger is directed at your family, friends, or coworkers, it needs to be managed and expressed in a healthy way:

- Start with what we call the "discomfort caveat" when you wish to communicate rage or any other negative emotion. Make it apparent to others that you are experiencing strong emotions and that it is more difficult for you to communicate clearly than normal. Apologize ahead of time, not for your feelings or actions, but for the probable lack of clarity in how you are going to say it.

  The purpose of the discomfort caveat is to de-escalate the situation and prevent the person from becoming defensive. When someone understands that you are uncomfortable and that the talk is challenging for you, they are more likely to listen with empathy to what you have to say.

- You might be able to write what you cannot say. Make a list of how you are feeling and how you wish to react. It can help you calm down and examine the events that led up to your feelings if you write them down. An anger management notebook is a tool that can be used to help people manage their anger. When we are furious, we frequently suffer a form of mental "fog" in which our ability to think is hampered. Writing in an anger management notebook assists the brain to focus its ideas by allowing it to express itself in a thoughtful and focused manner. Even simply "reporting" what made you angry or how it made you feel might help you regain control of your mind and emotions.

Simultaneously, simply writing about furious feelings and who or what triggered them is not enough to achieve a sense of closure and long-term control.

An anger management notebook should have structure and emphasis beyond filling up blank pages with tales of slights, hurts, and frustrations to make that kind of improvement.

There is no one approach to creating an anger management journal. However, there are three critical elements for maximum efficiency and ultimate peace of mind:

> **Self-Acknowledgment:** There is no way to find a healthy remedy before a person recognizes that there is a problem. This is not to say that your article in your anger management journal has to read like a confession of a transgression.

>> Instead, it is useful to remember two things:

>>> 1. A description of your anger in terms of an emotional reaction (including who or what was involved, when or where it occurred, and how or why your anger was triggered)

2. The circumstances in which you felt angry, e.g., who or what was involved, when or where it occurred, and how or why your anger was triggered (use of profanity, physical response, yelling, etc.)

You are validating yourself with this acknowledgment, and you are allowing yourself to perceive the circumstance and your anger with greater clarity with this perspective. Learning and growth emerge through acknowledgment and the resulting perspective.

➢ **Self-Compassion:**

Many people who are naturally furious focus their wrath on themselves, resulting in a devastating and exhausting cycle of resentment and regret. That is why writing about self-compassion in your anger management journal is crucial. This is not to say that you should wipe the slate clean or ignore any bad effects of your anger. Instead, self-compassion is a journaling approach that allows you to break the cycle of anger and regret. You can write in your notebook that everyone gets furious and makes errors and that you are working on regulating your emotions and getting control of your anger.

This is a process, and writing such reminders in your journal can help you to be more open to receiving and giving compassion and forgiveness. Compassion and forgiveness relieve the giver as well as the receiver of their burdens. That is one of the reasons there are so many remarkable quotes on letting go of grudges and anger. Self-compassion and self-forgiveness strengthen our abilities to show compassion and forgiveness to others, easing our emotional burden.

> **Mindful Action:**

Journaling about thoughtful/mindful action will help you feel more at ease and move forward. This does not imply you have to come up with a strategy to fix or mend the outcome of your anger, but it might be a good idea on occasion. Creating an entry that reflects thoughtful action, on the other hand, should contain a coping method other than rage. You may, for example, look at your self-compassion and write down the reaction you wish you had instead or an idea for how to remind your future self to halt and breathe before allowing anger to overwhelm you. Overall, this part of the journaling process will provide you with a sense of closure or resolution, allowing you to move on from the circumstance and your angry reaction.

If those sentiments return, or if you find yourself caught remembering and reliving specific events that made you angry, go back to this section of your entry and remind yourself to keep moving forward in your activities rather than going backward and interrupting your progress.

- Improve your communication abilities. Being overly angry and violent can make it difficult to effectively communicate your feelings and views. People may be preoccupied with your rage and find it difficult to hear what you are saying. On the other side, if you can express your anger by speaking assertively and respectfully about what has made you furious, others are more likely to understand you.

Being assertive entails sticking up for oneself while also respecting the views of others. It may be able to:

> ➢ Facilitate communication
>
> ➢ Avert tense situations from getting out of control
>
> ➢ Boost your self-esteem and connections

It may not seem easy at first to learn to be assertive, but here are some things to try:

> ➢ Consider the end result you wish to achieve. What irritates you, and what would you like to change? Is it sufficient to simply state your grievance?
>
> ➢ Be as precise as possible. For example, you may begin your remark with, "I am upset with you

because..." Using the term "I feel" avoids assigning blame and makes the other person feel less attacked. Respectful and specific communication is essential. Instead of saying, "You never do any housework," say, "I'm disappointed that you left the table without offering to help with the dishes."
> Listen carefully to the other person's response and try to comprehend their viewpoint.
- Be mindful when the conversation goes off the rails, and try to notice when this happens. If you find yourself becoming enraged, you should return to the conversation at a later time.
- Permit yourself to halt for a time when you are upset, even if someone is waiting for a response. You can even tell them that you are deliberately slowing down the situation. Rather than making quick decisions, choose to make good ones. Pauses, deep breaths, and periods of reflection exercise more power and control than rapid-fire replies when you are angry. If slowing down makes you feel less upset, that is terrific, but that is not the point. In an emotionally charged circumstance, this is about providing oneself more options to select from.
- It is simple to pass judgment on others; yet, empathy requires time and effort. It is intellectually closed-minded and lazy to make judgments and labels. When you are upset, take a step back and consider if something from your everyday routine is making you angry. It could be anything as simple as adjusting your commute to work or your everyday tasks; a small

change here and there can make a significant difference. But, in order to avoid worry, do not go too fast; instead, do things slowly.

- We have a tendency to say hurtful things or phrases to someone simply because we are angry. To avoid this, consider rehearsing what you are about to say so you do not get the same reaction the next time.

- When you are upset, it is evident that you do not have control over your words. As a result, if you are irritated by something, it is best to refrain from speaking. Most of the time, keeping your mouth shut works well. You will suffer a great deal if you choose to talk over being silent. You need to treat the other person fairly and rationally. This strategy will give you the 'Freedom to Choose' your answer while also improving your self-esteem in the long run. When you refrain from passing judgment on others, you are less inclined to pass judgment on yourself.

- Throwing something can help reduce stress and be useful in the short term. Do you have a yard? If you have enough room, get out there with a ball or some rocks to throw. Alternatively, break anything you wanted to get rid of, such as a mug or an old piece of rubbish. If that is not an option, get inventive and hurl anything soft (such as a roll of toilet paper or balled-up socks) against a blank wall or into the woods.

- Consider yourself a chess player. Consider how the other person will respond and how the scenario will look two moves from now before deciding on a plan of action. Continue on your current journey if everything appears to be in order. Consider an alternate behavior, picture how they will respond, and analyze this scenario if it appears to be bad.

- When you are feeling enraged, yelling into your pillow can be immensely cathartic and help you get out of your rage. If you are at work and have a few minutes to spare, your car is also a viable choice.

- Rather than focusing on what made you angry, focus on resolving the current problem. Is your child's strewn-about room driving you insane? Close the door behind you. Is your boyfriend always late for dinner? Plan your meals for a bit later in the evening — or agree to dine alone a couple of times per week. Remind yourself that anger is not going to solve anything and may even make things worse. If you believe you can change your existing position, the first step is to accept responsibility for your current condition. Proactive people acquire a solution-oriented mindset over time and thus spend less time in the first stage of rage.

- Do not harbor a grudge against anyone. Forgiveness is an extremely effective weapon. Allowing anger and other bad emotions to overpower happy emotions might lead to you being swept up by your own bitterness or sense of unfairness. However, if you can forgive someone who has offended you, you may be able to learn from the event while also strengthening your friendship.

These are the six vital steps that can help you manage your anger and lead a calm, peaceful life.

Chapter 4: Managing a Stressed Brain

Effective stress management can help you break the shackles that stress has on your life, enabling you to be healthier, happier, and more productive. What we want is a balanced life between relationships, work, fun, and relaxation, and to develop the strength to keep going when things get tough. Stress management has many methods of which some may work for you and some might not. That is why it is important to try different things and figure out what works for you.

Let's debunk some myths about stress before we move forward.

- **Stress is all around you, and there is nothing you can do about it.**

    True, stress is all around us, but you can manage your life such that it does not consume you. Setting priorities and fixing basic problems first before tackling more complex challenges is a good technique. When we are stressed, it is difficult to prioritize because all concerns appear to be equally distressing.

- **Only the most serious stress symptoms need to be addressed.**

    Minor symptoms, such as headaches or stomach acid, are early warning signs that your life is out of control and should not be overlooked. Do not wait until a serious stress symptom, e.g., a heart attack, to get help; it may already be too late. Making lifestyle changes, such as getting more exercise or eating a healthier diet will save you time, money and improve your health. Furthermore, if symptoms are not controlled, stress can quickly progress from acute to chronic.

- **Stress can be used as a motivator.**

    Although some people are motivated by stress, the benefits of motivation do not exceed the overall detrimental impact on health. Chinese community health professionals were asked about their work stress and motivation in connection to job satisfaction in a 2014 poll. This study discovered that work-related stress had a negative relationship with job satisfaction using two separate criteria.

    Short-term stress, particularly acute stress, can be motivating for some people. Acute stress improves an individual's alertness and helps them complete tasks such as reaching key deadlines. Acute stress may also assist people in performing at their best and thinking imaginatively about how to overcome difficulties. Stress is justified as a motivator in some situations.

    Chronic stress, however, which has long-term negative consequences, is less of a motivator and more of a burden. The long-term disadvantages of chronic stress on a person's physical, mental, and emotional well-being outweigh the benefits of acute stress.

- **If there are no signs or symptoms, there is no stress.**

    Just because a person does not exhibit stress-related signs or symptoms does not indicate that they are not stressed. Stress can quickly manifest itself in some people through behavioral changes or after traumatic occurrences. However, it may be incredibly difficult to tell if some are stressed, based on their conduct. Such people may appear normal and hide their tension successfully, but they are undoubtedly battling emotionally. Stress is usually manifested in two ways: cognitively and emotionally.

The following stress management methods can assist you in your stress-free journey:

4.1 Identifying Source of Stress

Exploring the reasons behind your stressed life is the primary step in stress management. However, figuring them out might not be straightforward. While significant stresses like moving, changing jobs, or going through a divorce are easy to notice, recognizing the origins of chronic stress can be very difficult. It is easy to misunderstand the part that your own feelings, ideas, and behaviors have in your stress levels. You may be continually worried about work deadlines, but the stress may be caused by your procrastination instead of the actual job obligations.

Examine your behaviors, attitude, and excuses to determine your true sources of stress:

- Do you think of stress as a part of your job or home life ("Things are always a little frantic around here") or as a personality trait ("I just have a lot of anxious energy that is all")?

- Do you rationalize your stress as transient ("I just have a million things on my plate right now"), despite the fact that you cannot recall the last time you took a break?

- Do you think your stress is caused due to other people or external circumstances, or do you think it is completely unexceptional and typical?

Your stress will stay out of your control unless you accept responsibility for your part in causing or perpetuating it.

Keeping a Stress Journal Will Help You Understand Your Problem

Keeping a notebook or diary is more than just a tool to record your ideas and experiences. Journaling is an effective stress alleviation practice, according to recent studies, and those who write in a diary or other notebook receive both physical and emotional advantages, perhaps extending their lives.

When compared to a control group, psychotherapy patients who were told to express their emotions through expressive writing had lower anxiety and depression symptoms and made more progress in psychotherapy, according to a recent study published in Psychotherapy Research.

Journaling may also assist you in reducing the amount of worry you experience. Another study published in the journal Behavior Modification found that expressive writing was linked to significant reductions in symptoms of generalized anxiety disorder, such as depression and worry.

How to do it?

Some people find putting pen to paper to be therapeutic, while others prefer typing their thoughts into a computer. There are even Web sites that allow people to journal privately online, such as LiveJournal and Penzu. Take some time for yourself in a peaceful, comfortable location where you will not be disturbed. Simply start writing and date your journal entry. When it comes to journaling, there are no hard and fast rules. You can write anything that you want. You can make your diary entry as long or as short as you choose.

Because no one but you will read your journal, do not worry about language or punctuation; simply record your thoughts as they occur to you. It is hard to understand where to start when writing a diary entry, but writing about your everyday activities is a good approach to get your thoughts flowing.

Remember that writing about your ideas, hopes, concerns, frustrations, and any other feelings you are experiencing in your notebook may be a terrific stress reliever, so try to write about them.

A stress journal can help you in identifying your regular stressors and how you deal with them. Keep a notebook or use a stress tracker on your phone to keep track of your stress levels. You will be able to see patterns and common triggers if you keep a daily log. Try to incorporate the following things to help you make sense of your stress:

- What was the source of your stress? (Guess if you are not sure)

- How you physically and emotionally felt?

- How you reacted to the situation?

- What you did to feel better?

4.2 Being Aware of Stress Signs

Although it may seem self-evident that you can tell when you are stressed, many of us spend so much time frazzled that we have forgotten what it is like when our nervous systems are in balance: when we are calm but alert and focused. If this describes you, listening to your body can help you detect when you are stressed. Your eyes may feel heavy, and you may lay your head on your hand when you are fatigued. When you are happy, it is easy to laugh. When you are stressed, your body will also let you know. Make it a practice to pay heed to your body's signals.

- **Examine your body**: Do you have stiff or aching muscles? Do you have a tight, cramped, or painful stomach? Do you have clenched hands or a clenched jaw?

- **Pay attention to your breathing**: Is it difficult for you to take a deep breath? One hand should be on your stomach, while the other should be on your chest. With each breath, notice how your hands rise and fall. Keep track of when you fully breathe and when you "forget" to breathe.

4.3 Finding Response for a Quick Stress Relief

Internally, the "fight-or-flight" stress reaction causes your blood pressure to increase, your heart to beat quicker, and your muscles to constrict. Your immune system is depleted as a result of your body's hard work. People, on the other hand, react to stress in different ways on the outside.

The greatest approach to relieve stress rapidly is to understand your stress response:

- If you are prone to being furious, overly emotional, agitated, or tense when you are stressed, you will benefit from stress-relieving activities that can calm you down.

- If you are prone to being sad, withdrawn, or spaced out when you are stressed, you will benefit from stress-relieving activities that are engaging and energetic.

Do you know about the "frozen" or the immobilization response?

A history of trauma is frequently linked to the immobilization stress response. When confronted with stressful conditions, you may feel completely trapped and powerless to act. Your goal is to reboot your nervous system and reactivate the body's natural "fight-or-flight" stress reaction in order to break free from your "frozen" position. Walking, swimming, sprinting, climbing or tai chi are all examples of physical activities that utilize both your arms and legs. Instead of focusing on your thoughts, concentrate on your body and the feelings you feel in your limbs as you move. This mindfulness component may assist your nervous system in becoming "unstuck" and moving forward.

Use Your Senses

You must first determine which sensory experiences are most beneficial to you. This may necessitate some trial and error. Keep track of how quickly your stress levels decrease as you use different senses. Also, be as accurate as possible. What is the exact sound or movement that has the most impact on you?

Explore a range of sensory experiences so you will always have a stress-relieving tool no matter where you are. The following samples are meant to serve as a starting point. Allow your mind to run wild as you come up with new things to test. You will know when you have found the proper sensory technique.

- **Smell**
    - Light a scented candle.
    - Take a whiff of roses or another flower.
    - Apply your favorite cologne or perfume.
    - Breathe pure, fresh air outdoors.

- Try different essential oils.

- **Sight**

    - To spice up your workspace, add a plant or flowers.
    - Take a look at a treasured photo or memento.
    - Enjoy nature's splendor in a garden, on the beach, in a park, or at your own home.
    - Close your eyes and imagine a relaxing and refreshing environment.
    - Colors that uplift your spirits should be all around you.

- **Taste**

Slowing down and indulging in a favorite treat can be incredibly relaxing, but mindless eating will just add to your waistline and stress. The idea is to enjoy your sense of taste in proportion and with awareness.

    - Take a small piece of dark chocolate and enjoy it.
    - Take a piece of sugarless gum and chew it.
    - Sip a cup of tea or coffee, or a cool beverage
    - Enjoy a crunchy, healthful snack (celery, carrots, or trail mix.)
    - Take a bite out of a perfectly ripe peach.

- **Touch**

- Pet a cat or a parrot
- Wrap yourself with a blanket to keep warm.
- Keep a reassuring object in your hands (a stuffed animal, a favorite memento).
- Wear clothing that is gentle on the skin.
- Give yourself a hand or neck massage.

- **Sound**
    - Listen to something that is peaceful or uplifting.
    - Listen to the sounds of nature: crashing waves, rustling trees, and birds singing.
    - Wind chimes can be hung near an open window.
    - Purchase a tiny fountain for your home or business to enjoy the relaxing sound of running water.

Vocal toning, as odd as it may sound, is a technique for lowering the stress chemicals adrenaline and cortisol. Before a meeting with your employer, try sneaking away to a quiet spot for a few minutes of toning and watch how much more focused and relaxed you feel. It works by working out the inner ear's small muscles, which help you catch the higher frequencies of human speech that convey emotion and reveal what someone is actually trying to say. You will not only feel more at ease in that encounter, but you will also be able to understand what he is trying to say.

How to do it?

Simply produce "mmmm" sounds with your teeth slightly apart and lips together while sitting up straight. Change the volume and pitch until you feel a pleasant vibration in your face and eventually in your heart and stomach.

If you are having problems figuring out which sensory techniques work best for you, what else can you do?

Look for inspiration anywhere you can, from your daily surroundings to recollections from the past.

- **Observe:** Observing how others cope with stress might provide you with useful information. Baseball players frequently chew gum before taking the field. Ask your friends how they manage to keep focused under stress.

- **Parents:** Consider how your parents vented their frustrations. After a long stroll, did your mother feel more relaxed? After a long day at work, did your father work in the yard?

- **Memories:** Consider how you used to de-stress as a kid. Tactile stimulation could be beneficial if you have a blanket or plush animal. Before an appointment, wear a textured scarf around your neck or bring a piece of soft suede in your pocket.

- **Imagination:** Try just visualizing vivid sensations when you are stressed. The same relaxing or invigorating impacts on your brain as seeing your baby's photo will occur when you imagine her face. You will never be without a rapid stress alleviation tool if you can imagine a strong sensation.

4.4 Making Use of the 4 A's of Stress Management

Stress is a natural nervous system response but some stressors happen at predictable times, e.g., during an office meeting, your commute to work, or a family gathering. You can choose handling predicted stressors in two ways: change your response or adjust the issue. It is useful to keep in mind the four A's while choosing one of the options in any situation:

1. **Avoid Undue Stress**

    It is unhealthy to avoid managing a hard situation. There are many stressors we can get rid of from our life despite believing otherwise.

    - **Avoid people who stress you out:** Restrict the amount of time you spend with someone who routinely generates stress in your life, or end the connection.
    - **Learn to say "no:"** Make boundaries and respect them. Be it your professional or personal life, biting more than chewing is a major reason for stress. Know the difference between "musts" and "shoulds" and telling "no" to take on unnecessary work when possible.
    - **Reduce your to-do list:** Observe your obligations, everyday chores, and timetable. If you feel like you have too much on your plate, move non-essential chores to the bottom of the list or delete them altogether.
    - **Take command of your surroundings:** Go for a longer but less busy route if traffic is stressful for you. Turn off the television if the news makes you

nervous. If a visit to the grocery store bothers you, shop on the internet.

2. **Alter the Situation**

   Try to change a stressful situation if you cannot prevent it. For example, changing the way you interact and function in your daily life.

   - **Express your emotions instead of hiding them:** You should be more assertive and share your concerns in a respectful and open manner if someone or something is troubling you. Say up front that you only have ten minutes to talk if you need to prepare for an exam and your talkative roommate just got home. If you do not share your emotions, bitterness will grow and raise your stress levels.

   - **Make a well-balanced schedule:** Make an effort to strike a balance between family and job, social engagements and alone pastimes, daily duties, and downtime. Burnout is caused by all effort and no leisure.

   - **Be prepared to compromise:** If you ask somebody to modify their behavior, show them that you are ready to change your own. It will be more probable that you will reach a happy medium if you are both ready to compromise a little.

3. **Adapt to the Stressful Situation**

   Change yourself if you cannot change the stressor. By altering your expectations and attitude, you can adjust to difficult events and restore control.

   - **Look at the bigger picture:** Examine the situation from a different perspective. Will the issue make a difference in a month? Is it worth getting stressed about? If you think the answer is no, you should devote your efforts and time to do something else.

   - **Reframe problems:** While you are in a tough position, look at things from a more positive perspective. Do not be annoyed by a traffic delay but consider it a chance to enjoy some alone time or listen to your favorite radio station.

     - **Practice gratitude:** When you are feeling stressed, take some time to think about all the things you feel grateful for in your life. It can also include your own abilities and characteristics. This simple method can help you in keeping a clear viewpoint on your life.

     - **Adjust your expectations:** Perfectionism is another major stressor that you can leave behind. Stop expecting perfection. Have appropriate expectations for others and yourself, and try to accept some things as "good enough."

4. **Accept the Situation**

   Stress is unavoidable in some situations. Stressors as the death of a loved one, national recession, or serious sickness are impossible to avoid or change. Accepting things as they are, is the greatest method to cope with stress in such situations. Acceptance is challenging, but it is easier in the long run than fighting a circumstance you cannot change.

   - **Look for the silver lining:** When confronted with huge obstacles, strive to see them as chances for personal development. Reflect on and learn from your mistakes if your poor decisions contributed to a stressful scenario.

   - **Do not try to control what you cannot control:** Many things in life are beyond our control, especially other people's actions. Instead of worrying about them, concentrate on the things you can control, such as how you respond to challenges.

   - **Feel free to express yourself:** Even if there is nothing you can do to change the unpleasant circumstances, expressing what you are going through can be quite relieving. Make an appointment with a therapist or talk to a trusted friend.

   - **Learn to forgive:** Recognize that we live in an imperfect world where people make mistakes. Let go of your resentments and wrath. By forgiving and moving on, you can free yourself from negative energy.

4.5 Making Time for Fun and Relaxation

You may lessen stress in your life by carving out "me" time in addition to taking charge and maintaining a positive attitude. Do not get stuck in the hustle and bustle of life to the point where you forget to look after yourself. Self-care is a requirement, not a luxury. You will be better able to handle life's stresses if you schedule time for pleasure and relaxation on a regular basis.

- **Make "Me" time:** Make time for rest and relaxation in your everyday routine. Allow no other duties to interfere. This is your chance to disconnect from all duties and re-energize.

- **Every day, do something you enjoy.** Make time for the things that make you happy, whether it is stargazing, playing tennis, or riding your bike.

- **Maintain your sense of humor:** Laughter aids your body's stress-reduction efforts in a variety of ways.

- **Start a relaxing routine:** Yoga, meditation, and deep breathing are examples of relaxation practices that trigger the body's relaxation reaction, which is the opposite of the fight or flight or mobilization stress response. Your stress levels will drop as you learn and practice these techniques, and your mind and body will become quiet and centered.

4.6 Learning to Connect with Others

Spending meaningful time with another human being who makes you feel understood and safe is incredibly relaxing. Face-to-face interaction, in fact, sets off a chain reaction of hormones that counteracts the body's defensive "fight-or-flight" response. It is a natural stress reliever from nature. So, make it a point to contact family and friends on a regular basis—and in person.

Remember that the individuals you talk to, do not have to be able to help you deal with your stress. Simply put, they must be good listeners. Also, do not let fears of appearing weak or burdensome keep you from speaking up. Your trust will be appreciated by those who care about you. It will only serve to deepen your relationship.

Of course, having a close buddy to lean on when you are stressed is not always practical, but you can strengthen your resistance to life's stresses by cultivating and maintaining a network of close friends.

4.7 Making Quick Stress Relief a Habit

Midst of crisis, it is difficult to remember to use your senses. It will feel simpler at first to just give in to the pressure and stiffen up. However, using your senses will become second nature over time. Consider how you would learn to drive or play golf. It takes more than one instruction to master a skill; you must practice until it becomes second nature. Though you do not tune in to your body during difficult circumstances, you will eventually feel as if you forget something. Here is how to turn it into a habit:

- **Identify and target:** Consider one low-level stressor, such as commuting, that you know will occur multiple times each week. Make a promise to yourself to always attack that stressor with immediate stress reduction. Target a second stressor after a few weeks, and so on.

- **Begin small:** Start with a predicted low-level source of stress, such as making sitting down to pay bills or dinner at the end of a long day, instead of testing your rapid stress relief techniques on a high-level source of stress.

- **Enjoy the process:** If something is not working, do not push it. Continue until you have discovered what works best for you. It should be enjoyable as well as notably relaxing.

- **Experiment with sensory input:** Bring a scented handkerchief one day, chocolate the next, and movement the third day if you are practicing rapid stress alleviation on your commute to work. Experiment until you come up with a clear winner.

- **Talk about it.** Informing friends or family members about the stress-relieving techniques you are experimenting with will assist you in incorporating them into your daily routine. As an extra benefit, it will almost certainly spark a lively discussion: everyone can relate to the subject of stress.

4.8 Managing Your Time Better

Poor time management can lead to a great deal of anxiety. It is difficult to be calm and focused when you are overworked and lag in the schedule. Plus, you will be tempted to avoid or reduce all of the good activities you should be doing to manage stress, such as socializing and getting adequate sleep. There are various methods for you to improve your work-life balance.

- **Do not take on more than you can handle**: Avoid scheduling events consecutively or trying to cram too much into a single day. We all too often underestimate the length of time it will take to complete a task.

- **Make a list of tasks:** Make a list of the things you need to complete and prioritize them. Prioritize the high-priority tasks first. Get it over with as soon as possible if you have anything really unpleasant or stressful to undertake. As a result, the rest of your day will be more enjoyable.

- **Break down tasks into manageable chunks:** Make a step-by-step strategy if a major undertaking becomes daunting. Rather than tackling everything at once, focus on one reasonable task at a time.

- **Assign responsibilities to others:** You do not have to do everything yourself at home, school, or at work. Why not delegate the duty to others if they are capable of doing so? Allow yourself to let go of the desire to be in charge of or oversee every detail. In the process, you will be releasing unnecessary stress.

4.9 Making Exercise a Habit

When you are stressed, exercising is most probably the last thing you want to do but physical activity is a great stress reliever, and you do not have to spend hours in the gym or be an athlete to benefit from exercise. Exercise releases endorphins, which make you feel good, and it can also be a fantastic way to get away from your daily troubles. People who exercise regularly are improbable to suffer from anxiety than those who do not. There are several causes for this:

- Exercise reduces stress hormones in your body, such as cortisol, in the long run. It aids in releasing endorphins, which are feel-good chemicals that also work as natural painkillers.

- Exercise can help you have a better night's sleep, which can be impaired by anxiety and stress.

- Regular exercise can help you feel confident in your body and competent, which can help you feel better mentally.

While you will gain the most benefit from a minimum 30-minute-long exercise on a regular basis, it is fine to progressively increase your fitness level. Even small acts can add up to a lot. What you need to do is to get up and start. Here are some simple methods to fit exercise into your daily routine:

- Take a walk with your pet.

- To get to the store, walk or ride your bike.

- Park the car at the end of the parking lot and walk the rest of the distance.

- Instead of taking the elevator, use the stairs at home or at work.

- Play an activity-based video game or Ping-Pong etc., with your children.

- As you work out, pair up with an exercise buddy and cheer each other on.

While any type of physical activity can assist relieve stress and tension, rhythmic activities are particularly beneficial. Walking, swimming, running, tai chi, cycling, and aerobics are all good options. But whatever you do, make sure you enjoy it so you will be more inclined to remain with it.

Make an effort and pay attention to your body and the physical (and occasionally emotional) sensations you feel as you move while exercising. Consider how the sunlight or air feels on your skin or how you can coordinate your breathing with your motions. Including this mindfulness, component will help you break out from the negative mental cycle that often comes with overwhelming stress.

4.10 Changing Your Lifestyle

Some other healthy lifestyle choices coupled with regular exercise can help you become more resistant to stress.

- **Maintain a balanced diet:** Be attentive to what you consume because well-nourished bodies are better at coping with stress. Start your day off correctly with breakfast, and eat nutritious, balanced meals throughout the day to keep your mind clear and your energy up.

A bad diet can make you more receptive to stress. Emotional eating and grabbing for high-sugar, high-fat foods may bring a short-term sensation of relief, but they will only add to your long-term stress. Potato chips and cookies, for example, can trigger a blood sugar increase. When your blood sugar levels drop, you may feel more stressed and anxious. A balanced diet might help you deal with stress in the long run. Mood management and energy balance are aided by foods like avocado, eggs, and walnuts.

- **Avoid sugar and caffeine:** Caffeine and sugar give short "highs" that are frequently followed by a slump in energy and mood. You will feel more relaxed and sleep better if you reduce your intake of soft drinks, chocolate, coffee, and sugary snacks.

- **Avoid cigarettes and narcotics:** Self-medicating with cigarettes or narcotics may provide a quick fix for stress, but the relief is fleeting. Deal with difficulties directly on and with a clear mind, rather than avoiding or masking them.

- **Make sure you get enough rest:** A good night's sleep fuels both your intellect and your body. You will be more stressed if you are fatigued because it may cause you to think unreasonably. Even partial sleep deprivation has been found to have a substantial impact on mood in studies. Researchers from the University of Pennsylvania discovered that participants who were only allowed 4.5 hours of sleep every night for a week felt more worried, furious, depressed, and intellectually weary. The individuals' moods improved dramatically once they resumed normal sleep.

These ten steps can help you minimize and handle stress, so it does not interfere with living your best life.

Chapter 5: Activities for Keeping Anger and Stress at Bay

Anger is one of the primary human emotions and issues like stress and anxiety that can lead to difficulties if it gets out of control. Fortunately, mental health specialists have developed a range of approaches to dealing with them over time.

If you are naturally hot, you will never be completely relaxed, but you can get to a place where the worst of your anger does not ruin your life. Many of the ways that can assist you in keeping a distance from unhealthy anger and stress will be summarized in this chapter.

5.1 Activities for Hot Heads

Let's get started:

- **Accidental Pie**

You may assume your anger is less severe and less frequent than it actually is. The Accidental Pie approach will provide you with an outsider's view of your anger, allowing you to see it as it happens. This will make it easier for you to control it.
  - ➢ Draw a big circle on a sheet of paper to symbolize your complete day.
  - ➢ Consider your feelings and categorize them into two groups: negative chemical emotions and positive chemical emotions. Anger, aggravation, and petulance are examples of the first. Calmness, satisfaction, and friendliness are among the second.
  - ➢ Draw pie slices to show how much time you spend with the bad chemical emotions each day. Draw a slice every time you are angry.

➤ You will have a better notion of how your temper looks by the end of the week. How much of your day is swallowed by rage and other bad emotions?

For a more accurate assessment, repeat this practice for several weeks.

- **Progressive Muscle Relaxation**

    When you are angry, you could experience muscle tension, which is an indication of stress in the body. A progressive muscle relaxation practice may be helpful in calming you down. Each muscle group in the body is tensed and then relaxed one by one. It is suggested that you start your relaxation therapy with a breathing exercise and then work your way up from your feet.

    1. **Feet**

        ➤ Curl your toes under your feet and point them downward.

        ➤ Gently tighten your toe muscles without straining them.

        ➤ For a few moments, pay attention to the tension, and then let it go and notice how you feel. Repeat.

        ➤ Notice the difference between relaxed and tense muscles.

        ➤ From the foot to the abdomen, continue to tense and relax the leg muscles.

2. **Abdomen**

    ➢ Tighten your abdominal muscles gently, but not too much.

    ➢ Take a few moments to notice the tension. Then let go and feel how relaxed you are. Repeat.

    ➢ Realize the difference between strained and relaxed muscles.

3. **Shoulders and Neck**

    ➢ Lift your shoulders up towards your ears gently. Do not overstretch.

    ➢ Feel the tension for a few moments, and then release it. Repeat.

    ➢ Take note of the difference between tense and relaxed muscles.

    ➢ Concentrate on the neck muscles, tensing and then relaxing them until they are completely relaxed.

- **Jumping Rope**

    Jumping rope is a high-intensity workout that needs concentration. The perk of this exercise is that it swiftly raises your heart rate and burns calories. It also necessitates the use of very minimal equipment. For less than $15, you can acquire a basic rope or a comprehensive system with app-based workouts and weighted ropes. Jump rope workouts may include moves like the running step, double foot jump, double under, or high step, which force you to focus on your feet instead of your anger.

- **Tai Chi Chuan and Yoga**

    Blood pressure has been demonstrated to be reduced by mind-body techniques such as yoga and Tai Chi Chuan. In fact, research comparing yoga to walking discovered that yoga was more helpful in improving mood and lowering anxiety than walking. So, if you are seeking a strategy to settle down when you are angry, one of these practices might be worth a try.

    Tai Chi

    Tai chi is a sort of martial art that originated in China, yet it is not hostile in nature. Instead, it is a succession of flowing movements and self-meditation. If you find yourself fired up and agitated, the gradual rhythm of the movement may help you calm down and lower your pulse rate.

Tai chi has many styles, but there are smartphone apps and online tai chi classes that can assist you if you are just getting started. The Tai Chi Foundation also has various instructional videos and may assist you in finding a local class.

Yoga

When you are feeling angry, you might want to try one of the many various forms of yoga available.

- Hatha yoga is a slower, gentler kind of yoga.
- Power and vinyasa yoga move at a faster pace and provide a more intense workout.
- Bikram yoga is done in a warm environment, which makes it challenging to concentrate on certain postures for the whole 90-minute class.

There is even a style of yoga specifically developed to help people vent their rage. "Rage Yoga" is available at facilities around the United States and Canada, or you can take a session online. If you are performing yoga at home, all you need is a yoga mat and some space, regardless of which practice you select.

- **Walking**

    Walking has a number of health advantages, like improved cardiovascular health and a lower chance of chronic diseases, e.g., type 2 diabetes.

    A single bout of walking (only 10 minutes) was found to lower aggression and anger in young adults in one study, though not statistically significant.

    In another study, 35 overweight participants who participated in a 12-week walking program experienced lower levels of reported anger, as well as reduced anxiety, weariness, depression, disorientation, and total emotional distress, when they walked 10,000 steps per day.

- **Anger Management Apps**

    Mental health apps are accessible and portable, and they can provide useful interventions at any time. Three of my favorites are listed here.

    > **Headspace** is a popular app that encourages people to practice mindfulness and meditation. Such strategies are very successful in helping us regain our composure and look at our emotions objectively, including anger.

    > **Happify** provides evidence-based stress management and life difficulties solutions. This software encourages users to develop new

healthy behaviors that will help them enhance their mental health and manage their anger.

> **Calm** is a well-liked application that can help you cope with stress and anxiety by encouraging you to maintain a calm attitude in difficult times. Use the tool to help you find a better balance in your life, manage anger and stress, comprehend connected emotions, and adopt a more positive, healthier view.

Moving forward, let's discuss how to calm your stress.

5.2 Activities for Stress Heads

Here we go:

- **Guided Imagery**

    It is similar to having a mental vacation. It may include visualizing yourself in your "happy place," such as listening to the waves, sitting on a beach, smelling the sea, and feeling the soft sand beneath your feet.

    You can practice guided imagery by listening to a tape of someone walking you through a serene scene. You can also practice guided visualization on your own once you have learned how to do it.

    Just close your eyes for one or two minutes and imagine yourself in a serene setting. Observe all of the sensory experiences you would have and allow yourself to feel as if you are there in person. Open your eyes and come back to the current time after a few minutes.

- **Circuit Training**

    With short pauses in between, circuit training contrasts weight-training routines with cardio. As a result, you will get a high-intensity workout that gives you the same benefits as lengthier workouts in less time (30 minutes or less). It is short, and it boosts your body's endorphin levels, which lifts your spirits. Even better, you would not have to worry about finding enough time to exercise.

- **Meditation**

    Short-term and long-term stress management is both provided by meditation. Meditation has many types to explore, each with its own set of benefits. You may spend a few minutes practicing mindfulness, which is being present in the moment. You can come up with a mantra to repeat in your head while taking calm, deep breaths. Simply focus on what you hear, see, taste, feel, and smell.

    You would not be able to linger on something that has already happened, and you will not be able to be concerned about something that will happen in the future if you are focused on the present. Mindfulness and meditation take practice, but they can help you reduce stress by bringing you back to the present moment.

- **Self-Massage**

    You probably already know how beneficial a professional massage at a health club or spa can be for reducing stress, discomfort, and muscular tightness. You might not realize it, but you can get some of the same benefits at home or at work by self-massaging or exchanging massages with a loved one.

    Take a few minutes to massage yourself at your desk in between chores, on the couch at the end of a long day, or in bed before going to sleep to help you relax. You can use aromatherapy, scented lotions, or combine self-massage with deep breathing techniques or mindfulness to help you relax.

    How to do it?

    To reduce muscle tension, use a mixture of strokes. Use the edge of your hands to make delicate chops, or tap with your fingers or cupped palms. Apply pressure on muscular knots using your fingertip. Knead soft, long, gliding strokes across muscles. You can use these strokes on any portion of your body that is conveniently accessible. Try concentrating on your neck and head for a short session like this:

    > Knead the muscles at the back of your shoulders and neck to begin. Drum quickly up and down the back and sides of your neck with a loose fist. Next, work for little circles around the base of your skull with your thumbs. With your fingertips, gently massage the rest of your scalp. Then, moving from front to back and then across the sides, tap your fingertips against your scalp.

- Massage your face now. With your thumbs or fingertips, make a series of little circles. Pay special attention to the muscles in your forehead, temples, and jaw. Massage the bridge of your nose with your middle fingers, working outward over your brows to your temples.

- Last but not the least, close your eyes. For a brief time, put your hands over your face loosely and exhale and inhale slowly.

- **Body Scan**

    Breath attention is combined with progressive muscular relaxation in this method. Following a few minutes long of deep breathing, you concentrate on one section of the body or set of muscles at a time, mentally releasing whatever physical tension you may be experiencing. A body scan can assist you in becoming more aware of the mind-body relationship. This strategy may be less effective for you if you have recently had surgery that has affected your body image or if you have other body image issues.

- **Pilates**

    Pilates is a set of exercises that focuses on improving body awareness, core strength, and alignment. Pilates develops a bodily equilibrium that makes it difficult for tension to take hold. It focuses equally on lengthening and strengthening muscles. Pilates is well-known for relieving back and neck discomfort, which is another stress-related symptom. Pilates can be done on a "The Reformer" machine, which is usually only found at Pilates studios or on a mat on the floor.

- **Tennis**

    Tennis is a wonderful aerobic activity that can help you avoid numerous stress-related illnesses like heart disease and high blood pressure. Tennis also keeps you linked to others because you cannot play it alone, which is a vital component of stress reduction. Take classes to master the basics and good form if you are new to the sport. Many city parks provide low-cost lessons as well as local leagues. Consider joining a private tennis club if you play regularly (or want to). Many are less expensive than a country club, and you can join a tennis community.

I hope this concluding chapter of the book to be your friend in handling angry and stressful situations.

Conclusion

We thrive on competitiveness, performance, and perfection in today's society, which leads to an incremental increase in stress and anger. This approach causes harm that is generally overlooked. An unjust judgment or a scathing remark activates autonomic responses in our brains, which stimulate the fight, escape, or freeze instincts that were formerly vital for existence. However, the subconscious mind is unable to discriminate between genuine and imagined threats, and when we repress our response, the autonomic nervous system continues to convey that danger signal.

Anxiety, or the worry of future threats, causes tension, concerned thoughts, and physical responses such as elevated blood pressure. It may not always make sense, but it is a physiological fact. Unresolved anxiety leads to anger, the emotional reaction to someone or something you believe has purposefully done you wrong. Anger can be a result of frustration or a reaction to incivility or bullying.

Anger and stress can have a negative impact on our physical health if we are exposed to them for an extended period of time. It can boost our blood pressure, which can lead to various physical and emotional problems. Anger can also have an adverse effect on our relationships. Furthermore, as a result of excessive amounts of anger and stress, we can establish undesirable habits that become increasingly difficult to manage over time. Both of these consequences can make you feel more anxious. In this book, we tackle the issue of uncontrolled stress and anger. The first chapter explains the causes of stress and anger. Your brought-up, past experiences and present challenging situations can flare up your anger, or it can be caused indirectly by stress.

Financial problems, personal relationships, change, fear, uncertainty, workplace problems, perception and attitude, and unrealistic expectations are the common culprits of stress.

The second chapter deals with the psychology of stress and anger and their damaging effects. The fight-or-flight response, which is triggered by stress, is the body's reaction to a perceived threat or danger. The relaxation reaction is aimed to return systems to normal operation once the perceived threat has passed. However, in the event of chronic stress, the relaxation response is not activated frequently enough, and being in a near-constant state of fight-or-flight might harm the body. Anger, on the other hand, rises from the amygdala that detects threats to our safety and sounds an alarm when dangers are recognized, prompting us to take precautionary action. The amygdala is so good at alerting us to risks that it gets us reacting before the cortex (the part of the brain that deals with intelligence and judgment) can check if our response is reasonable.

Stress and anger not only affect our internal organs and systems adversely but also cause insomnia, depression, and anxiety, opening outlets for many other illnesses.

The third and fourth chapters are focused on strategies for anger and stress management. Getting ready for a change, exploring yourself, identifying triggers, being aware of anger warning signs, learning to calm yourself, and expressing anger healthily are some methods of anger management. Identifying stressors, being aware of stress signs, finding an appropriate situation, making use of the 4 A's of stress management, making time for relaxation, connecting with others, exercising, and changing your lifestyle are some of the stress management methods.

The fifth chapter provides practical exercises and mobile applications to tackle anger and stress. These concluding words include activities accidental pie, progressive muscle relaxation, jumping rope, tai chi chuan, yoga, guided imagery, circuit training, meditation, self-massage, body scan, Pilates, and much more.

I have developed this anger and stress management book from personal and professional knowledge and experience in an effort to help you understand your situation and fix it. If my book was able to achieve that, I am beyond happy for you. Please leave a review on Amazon.